A journey to the Highlands of Scotland : with occasional remarks on Dr. Johnson's tour

Mary Anne Hanway

A

URNEY TO THE HIGHLANDS

OF

SCOTLAND.

With Occasional Remarks

on

Dr. JOHNSON's TOUR:

By a LADY.

LONDON:

Printed for Fielding and Walker,

Nº 20, Pater-noster Row.

122

TO THE

RIGHT HONOURABLE

THE

EARL of SEAFORTH.

MY LORD,

THE timidity which natu-
rally attends a young au-
thor on prefenting her firft at-
tempts to the public is obvious; and will, I hope, plead
her excufe for the ambition of
wifhing your Lordfhip to pa-
tronize

tronize them; for, to whom indeed, could an inexperienced candidate for fame fo properly fly for fhelter, as to *him*, whofe tafte and approbation will give it *eclat*, and fuccefs, in the world, and whofe politenefs and candour will excufe the errors of a female and unpractifed pen?

The intention of the following work, is, to give a juft reprefentation of a country, that hath been honored by giving birth to your Lordfhip's illuftrious anceftors;

anceftors; in *that* point I flatter myfelf I have in fome meafure fucceeded. In point of diction, I may have failed; but had I the fkill of a Millar, or a Montague, it fhould have been employed on the fame fubject. I am, with the greateft refpect,

My Lord,

Your Lordfhip's moft obliged

and obedient humble fervant

THE AUTHOR.

a 2

PRE-

PREFACE.

THE following letters are selected from a correspondence, begun, continued, and completed, upon motives of amusement, invitation, and tenderness. I took up the pen, indeed, to prove what will, I believe, be found universally true upon all human occasions. Meditating an excursion into the interior parts of the kingdom of Scotland, I had scarcely lost sight of the towers of

a 3   London,

London, even at the end of my first stage, before I felt that, according to Mr. Pope,

" *Self-love, and social is the same.*"

We may transport our persons, I perceive, to the remotest regions of the earth: From Caledonia we may direct our rambles into the deserts of Arabia, but the mind still remains untravelled, and clings fondly to that dear, and domestic circle whom we have left over our own fire-sides, and whose prayers and wishes are for ever on the wing to keep pace with our migrations. As the chaise therefore ran rapidly along,

bearing

bearing me every moment farther from the scene of my accustomed conversation, and the beloved objects, by whose ingenuity they were supported, I resolved to make my journey in some measure compensate the fatigue of undertaking it. This, first suggested to me those pleasures which are allowed even to absence, the pleasures of the pen; accordingly, I resolved to travel rather critically than casually, rather to accommodate my friends with information than merely to gratify the greediness of vacant curiosity. The consequences were, I did not suffer the postilion to indulge his professional passion, to pass

briskly

briskly through any parts of cultivated country, or rattle rapidly over the pavement of towns, that were fertile of remark, but ordered him to go sentimentally; *In a word, I rode* pencil in hand, *employing myself in drawing a sketch of the landscape, whether of hill or valley, morass or mountain, as it lay before me; a task, not the less agreeable for its abounding in novelties; or for the various prospects which rewarded it.* To this vanity, indeed, *may be attributed the spirit which resisted the inconvenience of sometimes travelling over heaths of almost immeasurable sterility:* But to these, a

.gover

gayer and fairer complexion of country always succeeded, which, seconded by the hospitality every where shewn to me and to my party, an hospitality, which marks the characteristic feature of the kingdom, not only made amends for those occasional glooms which seemed to breathe the spirit of melancholy, from the surrounding barrenness, but gave to the whole that sort of chequer-work, which, inevitably mixes with every business, and every pleasure, in the circumscribed journey of Life. On my return to London, after I had reciprocally given and received the embraces of welcome, I

was

was not a little surprised, (and I am woman enough to own, not a little pleased) to find those running papers which were trusted to the post, very favourably received by those to whom they were addressed. Nay, how shall I escape betraying the symptoms of vanity, when I further observe that Lady * * * had taken the pains, by the clue which the knowledge of my connexions gave her, to obtain copies from every other correspondent, and to put the little bundle, thus affectionately collected, into the hands of a literary gentleman?

To

To cut *short* a preface that begins to threaten prolixity, I *must observe*, that an interview was *soon* appointed betwixt me and the gentleman alluded to.

The volume annexed to this very preface, *shews* the re*sult* of our con-ver*sation*. I was per*suaded*, that, if I had not done every thing which might have been performed, I had noticed *several* things worthy of being made public, which more laborious travellers, and *some* of tho*se* who ab*solutely* journeyed ex officio, had neglected, or overlooked. Thus en-

5   couraged,

couraged, and thus advised, I sat
soberly down to the business of tran-
scribing. The next step is obvious;
I was hardy enough to visit the
perilous path that leads to Pater-
noster-Row—I saw myself going to
the press—I caught up the first sheet,
and was really delighted—I collected
every fair proof as it came out,
and saw my letters swelling gra-
dually into a volume, with a new-
born rapture which always attends the
juvenile mind on such occasions—The
bookseller talked of advertizing, and
under the pressure of a thousand pains
and pleasures, I wrote this preface.

What

What remains to be said; the volume is just going into the world—I dare not proceed, I have done my best, and am therefore somewhat relieved. The public are generous, and I sollicit its candour for the first effort of a female pen, very accidentally brought forward to their tribunal.

THE

CONTENTS.

LET.

LETTER I.

To Lady Mary B———

Edinburgh, July 29, 1775.

I Now take up the pen (in obedience to my dear Lady Mary's commands when I left England) to give her some account of Scotland and its inhabitants; yet I cannot, at present, say much as to either, having only been a few days in the capital. Nothing need be said of the road between England and this place, it being so universally known, since the legislature thought fit to

B   form

form an act which hath rendered it
fo ufefully fafhionable to the happy
race of Hibernian heroes and Englifh
miffes longing to throw off the lead-
ing-ftrings of parental reftraint. For,
the glowing females of the prefent
generation are not to be tyed down by
either prudifh or prudential duties,
to fathers and mothers, or any fuch
antiquated doctrines.--No, forfooth,
liberty! dear liberty is the Ton; and,
fo, heigh for a chaife and pair, and
Gretna-Green; for *that* you muft
know is the place, where (notwithftanding the frigid feelings of the na-
tives) Hymen lights his hafty torch
for thofe, that ride poft to the land
of matrimony.—But the moft laugh-
able

able circumſtance is, what you may
depend upon as a fact, that, this
kind phyſician of eloping lovers,
is by vocation a blackſmith, who on
the ſight of a chaiſe throws down
his hammer, and runs to the church
to give his benediction to the ſighing
pair; I had not the pleaſure of ſeeing him, or his place of reſidence:
yet I muſt not forget to tell you,
that though they who viſit our
Vulcan, go, now and then, upon the
wings of paſſion, the blackſmith
himſelf makes it, uniformly, a mere
matter of buſineſs. When the con-
jugal *work* is brought to his anvil,
he always ſtrikes the iron while it
is warm, and often proves himſelf,

alas!

alas! but too able an artificer, at connecting the *links* of the matrimonial *chain*. Neither would I have you imagine, our quondam self-ordain'd prieft acts fo much out of *character* neither; for, confider in the firft place, that Vulcan himfelf was the fon of that very goddefs Hymeneal Juno, whofe peculiar province it was to prefide over the myfteries of the married pair : and, fecondly, that he was the hufband of the beautiful Venus, and, confequently, nearly related to the little God of Love himfelf. So that you fee, his random reverence of Gretna-Green may not only boaft poetical licence for purfuing his occupation, but alfo plead the

privi-

privilege of his family. From this *prolific foil*, we went acrofs from Morpeth to take a view of ALNWICK CASTLE, the feat of the prefent Duke of Northumberland, and formerly, of that renowned warrior the Earl of Percy, whofe death gave a fubject for the beft Old Ballad in the Englifh language. The caftle has been entirely rebuilt, but fo, as to retain its ancient appearance of plainnefs and ftrength—The ramparts which furround it, are mounted with cannon; the ftatues, formidably armed *cap-à-pee*, feem to frown protection on the battlements; and the folemn ftillnefs that invades the traveller, while he furveys the structure, produce upon the mind a very pleasing effect; nor does the edifice promise to the spectator's curiosity more gratification *without*, than he enjoys *within*.—— The interior apartments are large, and finished in an elegant stile; every room is decorated in the most magnificent and superb manner, and, what cannot always be said on the same subject, arranged and disposed with a taste that doth honour to the worthy possessors. But I will hasten to conclude, having, I fear, long since tired you: my next, shall contain some remarks on Edinburgh, and I shall then endeavour to atone for the tedious prolixity of my pre-

fent

fent addrefs. In the mean time (tho' I have crofs'd the Tweed) believe me to be yours with the utmoft fincerity.

LET-

LETTER II.

To Lady Mary B———

Edinburgh, August 5, 1775.

I Now design to answer my oblig-
ing friend's claim upon me by
giving her some account of this
place. It is, I am sensible, an ar-
duous task I have undertaken, to
attempt the description of a city
which has been displayed already by
others, so much more capable; but
the desire of friendship is a suffici-
ent excuse. On entering Edinburgh,
the metropolis of Scotland, the very
capital in which once resided her
kings; an Englishwoman is rather
struck

ſtruck with diſguſt, than pleaſure—
for the ſtreets are narrow, except a
very few of the principal ones ; and,
from the ſtupendous height of the
houſes, dark and gloomy ; and
what, in my opinion, moſt ſhocks
Engliſh delicacy, is, to ſee all the
ſtreets filled with the lower claſs of
women, that wear neither ſhoes nor
ſtockings ; nor can it fail to ſtrike
any female, with an air of poverty,
to whom ſuch ſights are unuſual.
But, ſo much has cuſtom rendered
it ſupportable, and even agreeable
to theſe people, that, I actually
heard a young Highland woman ſay,
ſhe thought the greateſt puniſhment
that could be inflicted on her was

the

the being obliged to wear fhoes; but, though fhe was now tolerably reconciled to them, fhe never could prevail on herfelf to bear the confinement of ftays.

The new town is built after Englifh models; but the houfes of the *old*, are moftly ten ftories high, fome fourteen: and the frequent rains that fall here, occafion it to be very dirty, and render it a truly difagreeable place to live in. Holyrood Houfe, once the palace, is a noble pile of building, has a number of fine apartments in it, which are occupied by feveral of the nobility. In Lord Bredalbane's there are fome

re-

remarkably fplendid full lengths by Vandyck; and by Sir Peter Lely, the Duke and Dutchefs of Lauderdale, and the Earl of Jerfey—to which are added fome beautiful views of his Lordfhip's feat at Taymouth, which I hope foon to fee, having heard very high encomiums on it.

In Lord Dunmore's, there is a fine piece, very large, faid to be done by Vandyck, of Charles the firft, and his Queen, going to ride, with the fky fhowering rofes on them; an odd idea of the painter, though not a bad emblem to hold up to a King, as it fhows, that the

faireft

faireſt flowers are planted with-
thorns. The moſt agreeable circum-
ſtances attending this place are its
pleaſant walks : the Coulton Hill, a
little way from the town, is charming, enjoying a beautiful, and almoſt unbounded proſpect both of ſea
and land ; it is the mall of the Scotch
ladies. I have many times ſeen this
circular walk graced with forms,
that could not fail to raiſe love in the
men, and envy in the women ; the
laſt, being indeed, the natural conſe-
quence of the firſt. I may venture
thus much to you, who have not one
ſpark of that baneful quality in
your compoſition, even though you
are a woman, and a beauty.

The

The ladies here, are, the great *sub-lime in beauty*, moft of their favou-rite tcafts being five feet eight, or even nine. Methinks, I hear you laugh, and fay, what chance ftands my little lively friend? Why, they look at me with as much wonder as did the Brobdignags at Gulliver, and fpare me, I fuppofe, out of com-paffion to my diminutivenefs : in my turn I am content, their beaus being much too *high*, to raife in me an afpiring expectation.

I had almoft forgot to mention the CASTLE, where they fhow you the room and bed, in which the un-fortunate Mary was delivered of

James

James the fixth—it has nothing elfe remarkable—but is literally built on a *rock*, and appears to be impregnable ; it would at leaft hold out a term full as long as the fiege of Old Troy; before this, you think, *my letter* will do the fame, which makes me haften to conclude myfelf yours, moft fincerely.

LETTER III.

To the EARL *of* C————

Glasgow, August 10, 1775;

I Should naturally wish to be ex-
cufed writing to a person of your
Lordship's known fenfe and judg-
ment, had I not experienced your
good nature equal to your other
perfections; but *that* it is, which en-
courages me to throw off diffidences,
and depend upon the leading quality of your character to plead my
excufe. The place of date fhews
you that I write this at Glafgow,
being on a tour to Inverary; this
town (Glafgow) is a very good one,
and

and ought to figure confiderably in the hiftory of *modern Scotland*; the houfes are well built, and the ftreets broad and well paved. There is an air of *metropolitan dignity* in it, (notwithftanding the cold look of the ftone houfes) which entitle it to a much greater fhare of the traveller's admiration, than even the capital of the country; för Edinburgh is not only dirty, difmal, and irregular, in many parts, but feems more contracted, and is built upon a lefs liberal fcale—Glafgow, hath alfo the great advantage of fuperior architectural uniformity; infomuch that, if a few unequal, petty cots were pulled down, and others correfpond-

corresponding with the modern plan
substituted in their stead, there
would not, perhaps, be in any part
of Britain (Bath excepted) a more
spacious, or a better arrangement of
buildings—It is, by far, the greatest
commercial town in the kingdom,
and that very mercantile spirit, pro-
duces those effects in the appearance of the people, which commerce
never fails to bestow,—industry, content, and opulence; whilst in Edinburgh, there is a poverty, and a sort
of northern misery in the very fea-
tures of the commonalty—*here*, on
the contrary they appear happy, and
debonair. Labour is sweetened by
the comforts that attend it, and the

C   exigen-

exigencies of *poverty*, are fupplied by the moft grateful means in the world—by the exertions of her own *diligence*; fuch will ever be the benefits arifing from the feats of trade, to every part of mankind. If your Lordfhip will pardon me a quotation, I fhould tell you that I am irrefiftibly tempted to throw out a few a-propos verfes written by a celebrated Scotch bard, on the bleffings in queftion — When a woman fets *her heart upon any thing*, you know, my Lord, 'tis not in nature, or argument, to make her eafy. In fhort, my dear Lord, I am fo poetically inclined, juft now, that I muft rifque them. Here they are.

Thefe

"" Thefe are thy bleffings, INDUSTRY! rough
   power!
Whom labour ftill attends, and fweat, and
   pain ;
Yet the kind fource of every gentle art,
And all the foft civility of life:
Raifer of human kind.
Hence every form of cultivated life,
Hence COMMERCE, brings into the public
   walk
The bufy merchant:
All is the gift of INDUSTRY : whate'er
Exalts, embellifhes, and renders life
Delightful———"

But to return from poetical defcriptions to plain matter of fact. The
college is a large handfome building; it looks equally venerable
and claffical. The library is a very
noble room with a gallery round it,

supported by pillars; there is likewife a very good collection of original pictures shewn here, with
which I was very agreeably entertained, though no virtuofo or con-
noiffeur. Here is the only cathedral
remaining entire in Scotland, which
the levelling fury of rapacious re-
formation luckily fpared; there is a
church under it, where divine fer-
vice is performed for thofe people
who think religion beft enforced,
by gloomy difplays and terrific appearances. Undoubtedly, this fub-
terraneous place of worfhip is happily enough calculated. For my
part, I never am fo thoroughly difpofed to indulge the feelings of devotion,

votion, as when she comes to me arrayed in the robes of a forgiving seraph, and, I conceive, terror and holiness, are ideas which can never be, at the same time, associated and reconciled. No, my Lord, that *religion* which is from *above*, is rational, benevolent, and smiling; but the piety, or rather the hypocrity, which *frowns* its votaries into penury, mortification and abstinence, is from *below*, and will never promote the felicity of man, or the honour of God. The black and dismal looks of this *Golgotha* strike horror in the beholder: nor, indeed, do the Scotch bestow any decorations on their churches, so that

they

they may fafely fay with Pope:

" No *filver* faints, by dying mifers
  given,

" *Here*, brib'd the rage of ill-requit-
  ed Heaven ;

" But fuch plain roofs as piety could
  raife,

" And only vocal with the Maker's
  praife."

There, my Lord, is a fecond quotation for you. How eafy and natural the gradation from one trefpafs
to another—The places of worfhip
being " made vocal with their Mak-
" er's praife," is certainly their greateft recommendation; yet, furely, if
it is the tafte of the times, to lead
us into vaft expences to ornament
          our

our private villas, it is but reafon-
able that, thofe ftructures which are
confecrated to the Deity fhould at
leaft *partake* of the fplendor, if our
ambition were not to *furpafs* it. The
only embellifhment, however *here*,
is the fable walls being daubed over
with white fpots, at which on my
expreffing wonder, our conductor
(with no appearance of ridicule in
his face) informed me, it was meant
as an emblem, to fignify *tears*. I am
certain thought I, if I ftay here much
longer it will have the effect of drawing fome *real* ones from my eyes:
" For, here fits Melancholy, and
   round her throws
" A death-like filence and a dread
   repofe."
C 4   A third

A third copy of verfes flipping from
my pen! Fie upon it—fure I am
poffeft by the very dæmon of poetry.
I dare not trouble your Lordfhip
with any more on the fubject leaft
the gloom become contagious, and
thofe vapours fhould invade your
Lordfhip, which have feized

   Your much obliged

    obedient Servant.

     L E T-

LETTER IV.

To Miſs ————

Glaſgow, Auguſt 11, 1775,

WITH the greateſt pleaſure, my dear ſiſter, did I receive yours at Edinburgh ; you deſire me to write to you, and like the reſt of my friends in England, tell me, you expect to be highly entertained with an account of all the places I ſee : Is not that making rather hard terms with me ? for, how can I be anſwerable, that, what gave me great pleaſure in viewing, will give an equal degree of pleaſure to you in deſcribing ? But take the follow-ing :

ing as a specimen.—In our way to this place, we took a view of Hamilton, the seat of the present Duke of that title; it is a noble pile of building—but, unfortunately, the architects who planned *this* seat, and most others in Scotland, chose, in obedience to the prevailing notion, " to wrap their talents in a napkin," by burying their houses in a bottom, rather than displaying them on an eminence. Thus, they lost a fine prospect; but their motive was evidently that of utility, designing by such an entrenchment, and fortification of surrounding hills, to shelter themselves from the winds, which are

are, without doubt, very keen and searching here in the winter.

The same passion of *immuring*, indeed, prevailed, formerly, in countries, where the same apology doth not offer itself in palliation of what we should now call, a *false taste*. Even in travelling through the several parts of *England*, (where the elements, tho' precarious, are yet by no means so generally tyrannical as in the bleaker and more mountainous countries,) one observes the remains of this propensity in our progenitors, to hide themselves behind an immensity of stone-walls, and of *inhospitality* concealing from

the

the traveller the chearful profpects
of a manfion-houfe, a park, or a
pleafure-ground.

Thanks, however, my dear, to the
fair and *open* temper of the times,
every thing is now fufficiently dif-
played; and, whatever charges may
be brought againft the moderns,
neither moralift, critic, or cynic
will, I believe, reproach them for
concealing their poffeffions; or, indeed
for veiling from the general eye either the beauties of building, the
ornaments of *horticulture*, (furely
I may in *my* journey, my dear, be
allowed one hard word) or the
graces of the perfon.—It is a very

fhew

ewy age, fifter, and fuch is, at pre-
nt, the prevailing fpirit, that I
now not any one fo antiquated, as
, hide a fingle fpangle of fplen-
our, on any account.

The gallery at Hamilton, is of a
eat extent, and there are many
her good rooms which are fur-
fhed with fome excellent original
iintings; one by Rubens, of Da-
el in the lion's den, efteemed a
pital performance. A ftrong faith
the Omnipotent difpofer of man-
nd, for his prefervation, is finely
preffed in the face of Daniel,
ough furrounded by thofe terrible
d ferocious animals, who appear

ready

ready to devour him, but are reftrained by an invifible power. The marriage-feaft by Paul Veronefe, is a very fine piece; Fielding, earl of Denbigh in his grey hair, a gun in his hand, and attended by an Indian boy, is efteemed one of the beft of Vandyck's portraits; it really appears to have life and action. It was, indeed, a noble proof of

" The living image in the painter's
     breaft,
" Whence, endlefs ftreams of fair
     ideas flow,
" Strike in the fketch, or in the
     picture glow."

A head, faid to be Anna Bullen's, very beautiful, dreffed in purple, edged

edged with ermine, drawn with a veil over her face, but so transparent, as not to conceal the beauties under it. There are a great number of other pictures equally worth notice; but I have mentioned more already, than I have been able to do justice to; so, will leave them to some future traveller, more capable of the task.

But I cannot quit the subject without telling you, that on looking at that admirable piece, Daniel in the lion's den, I could not help smiling to think, that, setting aside the company of the real lions, the sight of the picture would be capable

ble

ble of throwing a dozen of our modern poets into fits. About
the house, on an emi-
...telrault : it was in
a banquetting-houfe, it
s an extenfive, and beauti-
fu v of the country ; there is
a y fine ruin of an old caftle to
be een from the gardens, and one
of the moft romantic walks you can
conceive, through which we returned to Hamilton ; the water
gufhing through breaks in the op-
pofite rock, falls with a pleafing
noife into the river that rolls beneath
your feet, with a hanging wood
above ; which entertained us all the
way, with a concert by the winged
inha-

inhabitants of thefe Arcadian fcenes :
a charming place this, for a poet to
woo his mufe, or a lover to whifper
foft things to his miftrefs, efpecially,
as the blind urchin is totally driven
from cities. But I muft conclude;
the chaife is at the door ; I ftep into
it, to purfue our journey ; which
will, probably, be the occafion of
purfuing my curfory remarks.——
Meantime, believe me,

Ever

Yours.

LET-

LETTER V.

To LADY MARY B———

Loch-Lomond, August 13, 1775.

I Write this from a place, my dear Lady Mary, of which I am (to ufe a woman's word) *extravagantly* fond, being one of thofe rural, and romantic fpots which the Arcadian fwains were poetically fuppofed to enjoy in the Golden Age. The road between this and Glafgow is very pleafant; and in our way, we paffed by the obeiik that has been erected by a relation to the memory of the celebrated Smollet. I had literary curiofity enough, you may be

sure,

fure, to get out of the chaife to read the infcription, which, I expected, to find fenfible or pathetic: but, alas! as Goldfmith fays, by the venifon pafty, I was prefented with a pillar where the writing *was not*—it, in fact, having not a fingle letter en- graven, to acquaint the traveller, (as a trophy of fame) to whofe com- memoration it is facred. Where were the Mufes of a Beattie, a Home, a Richardfon, or an Ogilvie? Had they fo foon forgot, one of the greateft ornaments of their country? Or were they, even *after death*, jealous of that pofthumous reputation, which however great, cannot gratify the. object on whom it is beftowed? Poor

D 2 Smollet

Smollet lies without a verfe : This neglect is the more unpardonable, my dear Lady Mary, as the Doctor, in one of his lateft publications, fpeaks very handfomely of this very fpot. That the blufh of omiffion may be deepened in the cheeks of his fellow poets, I fhall tranfcribe his very fentiments on this fubject; not *only* indeed, for the above reafon, but becaufe *his fhort* defcription may ferve to elucidate mine, which is more exact and explicit. "We have fixed our head quarters," fays the Doctor in the expedition of Humphry Clinker, "at Cameron, a very neat country houfe belonging to Commiffary Smollet, where we

found

found every accommodation we could defire. It is fituated like a druid's temple, in a grove of oak, clofe by the fide of Loch-Lomond, which is a furprifing body of pure tranfparent water, unfathomly deep in many places, fix or feven miles broad, four and twenty miles in length, difplaying above twenty green iflands, covered with wood; fome of them cultivated for corn, and many of them ftocked with deer: they belong to different gen-tlemen, whofe feats are fcattered along the banks of the lake, which are agreeably romantic, beyond con-ception." But ftill, my dear Lady Mary, although our poet hath

D 3 thus

thus made Loch-Lomond,

"Live in defcription, and look
 green in fong;"

not a bard, I fay, hath had the
gratitude to beftow a few tributary
verfes. What a reflection then to
the bards of Caledonia, to let a
brother poet remain unfung! His
friend, no doubt, did all he could;
for, you know, it is in the power of
many a man to raife a monument
that cannot write an epitaph. But
peace to his manes! and may he
meet that recompenfing wreath of
bays in the Elyfian fhades, which
his countrymen feem not very
ready to grant him on earth!
Excufe this digreffion from *my* de-

6   fcription

fcription of Loch-Lomond, which, you will now confider as fupplemental to Smollet's. This beautiful piece of water, has (for I was very exact) *thirty* iflands on it, all finely fertile; fome have luxariant trees growing on them; and one in particular hath the ruin of a caftle, which being nigh the centre, adds greatly to the beauty of the profpect. It luckily proved a clear day, and we went all round them in Sir James Colquhoun's pleafure-boat, the proprietor of this pleafant, I had almoft faid paradifiacal fpot. I faw the floating ifland mentioned by Smollet; it is evidently a part of the *bank*, which the rapidity of the torrent has

forced

forced off and carried with it into the lake; it is not large, and often undulates from one fide to the other. Sir James, planted fome little trees on it, but they do not thrive, though the fod has a beautiful verdure. We landed on one of the iflands, which is planted with yew, and ftocked with deer: we faw a great many of them; and walked up a high hill that prefented us with a profpect too pleafing to be well defcribed by your correfpondent. Picture in your imagination the fun fhining with all its fplendour on the Loch, unruffled with the leaft wind, and thefe fairy ifles fcattered on the furface in " regular confufion:" On one fide

the

the woods, and corn fields in all
their luxuriance grow down the
flopes clofe to the margin of the
water; on the other Ben Lomond
rears his lofty head as if he bid defiance to thofe clouds, which, I
have feen hanging miles below its
top. This hill, at the end of the
Loch, is a wonder in its kind:
its fides appear a fine green; it is
fix miles from the bafe to the top:
I could have liked to have afcended
it, but found no one willing to ac-
company me on fo romantic a tour,
fo was obliged to content myfelf
with a diftant view of this magnificent object. Sir J— C—— told
me, there was a young Scotch lady
that

that walked up in the morning and returned to dinner without appearing tired :. I think I hear some fine lady amongst my own countrywomen, who affect to be tired to death with a couple of turns in the Mall, exclaim, Oh! what horrid, indelicate creatures must those women be that could *form* such a plan, much less *execute* it! But I know you will join me in despising the affectation of those females who think, because indulgent Fortune has thrown a coach in their power, they are not to make use of the gifts Nature has bestowed. At the end of Loch Lomond, as we stopped to bait, at a little inn, in our way to

the

the Duke of Argyle's, I saw upon
a pane of glafs very legibly cut by
a diamond, fome verfes by a poetical traveller, containing a very exact defcription of Ben Lomond.
Though the ufual fcratches upon
tavern windows will feldom bear
even reading, yet thofe were fo
agreeable an exception to the rule
of general nonfenfe, and indelicacy,
that I thought them worth tran-
fcribing; the trouble of which I
undertook at the coft of penciling
upon my knees. But as they were
fcarcely ever made public, they
may perhaps pleafe you, and that
will be a delightful recompence.

Verfes

Verſes on BEN LOMOND.

Written on a Window.

STRANGER, if o'er this pane of glaſs
     perchance,
Thy roving eyes ſhould caſt a caſual glance;
If taſte for grandeur, and the dread ſublime,
Prompt thee, Ben Lomond's fearful height
     to climb;
Here ſtop attentive, nor with ſcorn refuſe,
The humble rhimings of a tavern muſe:
For thee the muſe, this rude inſtruction
     plann'd,
Prompted for thee, her humble poet's hand.
Truſt not at firſt a quick advent'rous pace,
Six miles its top points gradual from the baſe:
Up the high riſe, with panting haſte I paſt,
And gain'd the long laborious ſteep at laſt.
More

Iore prudent thou, when once you pass the
　　deep,
With cautious steps, and flow, afcend the
　　steep.
Oh, stop awhile, oft tafte the cordial drop,
And reft, oh reft, long, long upon the top.
There hail the breezes, nor with toilfome
　　hafte,
Down the rough flope thy ufeful vigour wafte;
So fhall thy wond'ring fight at once furvey,
Woods, lakes, and mountains, vallies, rocks
　　and fea;
Huge hills, that heap'd in crowded order
　　ftand,
Stretch'd o'er the Weftern, and the Nor-
　　thern land:
Enormous groupes; while Ben, who often
　　fhrouds
His lofty fummit in a veil of clouds,
High o'er the reft, exulting in his ftate,
In proud pre-eminence, fublimely great:

　　　　　　　　　　　　　　　　One

One fide all aweful to the aftonifh'd eye,
Prefents a rife three hundred fathoms high :
Which fwells tremendous on th' aftonifh'd
     fenfe,
With all the pomp of dread magnificence.
All this and more fhalt thou with wonder fee,
And own a faithful monitor in me.

J. RUSSEL.

Adieu, my dear Lady Mary: And whilft I cenfure the female follies of the age we live in, may I improve by the virtues that conftitute *your* character, is the fincere wifh of

    Your much obliged friend,

      and obedient fervant, &c.

LET-

LETTER VI.

To the EARL *of* C——

Inverary, August 14, 1775.

I Have been for some days past, my Lord, on a pleasant tour through the Western Highlands. This is written from Inverary, the seat of the present Duke of Argyle, but which was originally the property of the Campbel family, and after that, inhabited by the wonderful and whimsical Colin, who is reported to have set fire to his house to gratify his ambition, of displaying

ing to a friend the grandeur of his equipage in the field. This superb modern building was begun by the *late* Duke, and finished by the *present*; it stands in a park surrounded by immense hills, planted, to their summit, with firs. Loch-Fine, an arm of the sea, rolls close to the town, which is all re-building with stone by the Duke; and will, when finished, make a handsome appearance. The castle is genteelly furnished in the present taste, and from the number of bedchambers, is capable of entertaining a numerous train; which provision, indeed, the gloominess of the situation must render very necessary; for,

for, they tell me, it rains here eleven
months out of the twelve, which,
I think, may be eafily accounted
for, from its near affinity to the
fea, and the mountains that furround it;, for, as a *learned* and
elaborate traveller, in his ufual
pomp of phrafeology with great *fcru-*
pulofity of *minute inveftigation* obferves,
" where there are many mountains,
" there will always be much rain,
" and the torrents pouring down
" into the intermediate fpaces, fel-
" dom find fo ready an outlet, as
" not to ftagnate, till they have
" broken the texture of the ground."
The philofophy as well as the
philology of this paffage, is, to be

E   fure,.

fare, very profound, and means, pretty near as much, as many other parts of this inveſtigator's viſionary journey: not that I mean, my Lord, invidiouſly to rob the gentleman of the praiſes due to him for ſe-veral *real* diſcoveries which are ſcat-tered through his publication: ſuch, for inſtance, as that, " *mountainous* " *countries are not paſſed without* " *difficulty*; that, *climbing is not always* " *neceſſary*; that, *what is not mountain* " *is commonly bog*, through which " bogs, *the way muſt be picked with* " *caution.*" Theſe ingenious and im-portant informations, have, I per-ceive, already attracted the ridicule of our acute Engliſh critics, and,

3   as

as the subject hath fallen in my way, I could not help joining the chorus of ironical approbation for the edifying remarks of the great D. J———, of whom, however, I must take leave at present, not without a promise to return again soon, and *bend a keener eye*, upon his *volume of vacancy*. The castle of Inverary is in a bottom, the great fault of all their houses in this country; for you do not know you are near any inhabited place, till you find your chaise at their gates. We have, unfortunately, been favoured with a specimen of the weather natural to the place, having been unable to walk out,

for

for some of the heaviest rains I ever
saw. I began to tremble—Heaven
forgive me! least the world was
once more destined to be de-
stroyed by a deluge; even now, my
Lord, it is pouring down in torrents. We shall quit it to-morrow,
" nothing loth," without penetrat-
ing any farther into the Highlands,
this way, and return by the same
road we came, which is, to me, not
a displeasing one, though the major
part that travel, are of a contrary
opinion: I cannot better describe it
than by saying, it strikes a pleasing
gloominess that I do not dislike,
being so new to me, who have only
been used to bowl away upon a

turn-

turnpike road in England. It is called Glencroe: the road has been rendered good by the foldiers; it lies in a glen between immenfe mountains, that rear their black and naked tops much above the clouds. I faw fome horfes that appeared cropping a miferable mouthful, half way to the top, which, from their heighth, did not appear bigger than fpaniels: My wonder was what the brutes could poffibly find to eat; but a Scotch horfe is not the niceft animal in the world, and will live any where. Perhaps, they have fufficient fagacity of inftinct, to imitate the frugal maxims of their mafters; and the pampered Englifh

E 3 horfes,

horses, and Englifh riders, are not
far enough North, and too much accuftomed to the foftening luxuries
of the South, to adopt that general
habit of oeconomy, which, from
the higheft to the loweft order of men
is here the characteriftic. I muft not
forget to tell you, there is a conti-
nuation of natural cafcades falling
all the way, which gives a grandeur
and fparkling fplendour to the
fcene, which render it awefully delightful. There is fomething ex-
quifite to me, even in the *cadence*
of a cafcade: as I liftened to it in
this captivating fpot, I really felt
my imagination expand, and if I
had any thing of the bard in my

com-

composition, this would have been the moment of inspiration. Alas! my dear Lord, the Muse would not come at my bidding, and I was obliged to recur to the description of one whom the Muse more highly favoured. *His* cascade is so 'like *mine* at Glencroe, and so much better painted than I could have painted it, that I scruple not to invite your acceptance of a transcription; though as I trust wholly to memory, not having the book with me, I may perhaps transcribe incorrectly. Should this be the case, you know what excuse is to be made for it.

E 4   "As

" At firſt, an azure ſheet it ruſhes broad :

" Then whitening by degrees, as prone it
    falls,

" Daſh'd in a cloud of foam, it ſends aloft

" A hoary miſt and forms a ceaſeleſs ſhower ;

" Then, falling faſt, from gradual ſlope to
    ſlope,

" With wild, infracted courſe, and leſſen'd
    roar,

" It gains a ſafer bed, and ſteals at laſt

" Along the mazes of the quiet vale."

It is now proper to acquaint
you, that, ſoon after our return to
Edinburgh, we ſhall purſue our
intended journey into Murrayſhire;
and if any thing occurs that I
think will be in the leaſt pleaſing

to

to your Lordſhip, I will continue to ſcribble.

I am,

with the greateſt reſpect,

your moſt obliged ſervant.

LETTER VII.

To the EARL *of* C———

Sterling, August 22, 1775.

I Resume the pen, my Lord, to let you know, we are once more in motion, having turned our backs on Edinburgh, and begun our journey into Murray. You desire me to continue writing, and to make my remarks on things as they strike me—You shall be obeyed; so when you are tired, do not complain. We yesterday dined at Linlithgow, famous for the remains of the palace,

where

where Mary Queen of Scots was born, but which has nothing now remaining except the outer walls. It appears from the roads a fine ruin; it was burnt in forty-five by the King's army. The next ſtage was Falkirk, and from thence to Sterling, where we lodged: We this day took the track of the rebel army, and were I to offer my opinion from the obſervations I have been enabled to make of the life and manners of this people, it would be, that, their ſo eaſily gaining followers, and poſſeſſing themſelves of theſe towns, is not at all ſurpriſing; ſince thoſe, who were well-affected to government, were ſo few, in com-

comparifon with that ignorant mul-
titude, which run with the ftream,
and are one moment ready to join
the Pretender's ftandard, and the
next, on fight of our troops to
difcard their new-acquired friends
and throw up their bonnets for
KING George.

" Some popular Chief
More noify than the reft, but cries halloo,
And in a trice the bellowing herd come out;
And one and all is the word;
They never afk for whom, or what they fight,
But turn 'em out, and fhew 'em but a foe;
Cry liberty, and that's a caufe of quarrels."

Is it then matter of wonder that
towns fhould yield, which had it
not

not in their power to make the leaſt
reſiſtance to this rabble of deſpera-
does? for *ſuch*, and not an army, it
might, with juſtice, be ſtiled. But
a truce with politics, they ill become a woman's pen; and I know
not a more ridiculous character than
a petticoat pedant, or politician.
Neverthelefs, being on the ſpot,
which, at that period, ſet all England in a tremor; I was led irreſiſ-
tibly to theſe conſequent reflections;
let this plead my excuſe. I this
morning took a view of STERLING
CASTLE, which ſtands on a very
high rock, fortified impregnably
by nature. Within its walls is a
ſquare building ornamented with
pillars

pillars refting on ftrange grotefque-looking figures. It was once the palace of feveral of the Scotch kings. From the ramparts of the caftle, you are prefented with one of the moft romantic and beautiful views in Scotland; you fee a vaft plain waving with yellow corn (now in all its beauty) adorned with woods, and watered by the river Forth; which though but four miles of water, by its various mazes and labyrinths, peninfula-like, covers twenty miles of ground, and appears, to a cafual obferver, not as one river, but a number of rivers. I think one of the greateft beauties that Scotland eminently poffeffes, is, their

many

many noble rivers, which is, a full
compenſation for that general want
of wood which is complained of by
unſatisfied travellers; that, are ſo far
from being contented with the proſpect before them, they muſt forſooth,
have towns and countries made on
purpoſe to pleaſe them, or elſe they
exclaim againſt art and nature, even
for preſenting them with that very
variety, which conſtitutes the greateſt entertainment. Nor do theſe
querulous gentlemen ſeem to reflect
that, if the face of the earth was
naturally uniform; if deſtitute of
that diverſity, which it derives from
the hill and valley, the barren heath,
and the blooming garden, there
would

would neither be any motive to ex-
cite the curiofity of the traveller,
nor, perhaps, any incentive for one
country to connect itfelf *commercially*
with another. But with refpect to
Scotland it is but in a few places
totally *denuded*. I mean not to infi-
nuate, like the pedantic Dr. J——,
that there are but two trees in one
county, and they *ftumpy:* Dr. J——
is a gentleman whofe ability and ve-
racity as an HISTORIAN, I muft beg
leave to call in queftion, in fpite of
that curious *adaptation* of high-flown
words, which he hath, with great
labour, jumbled together for the
edification of thofe good people that
travel in their clofets; to fuch only,

muft.

muſt his tour be addreſſed, ſince
thoſe who go the ſame road, will
ſoon be *convinced*, how falſe an account he has given of a country, to
the hoſpitality of whoſe inhabitants he
owns himſelf ſo much obliged. As a
theoriſt, I allow Dr. J— to be a very
moral man; but as a *practical
moraliſt*, at leaſt while on his tour,
I have as great an objection to him,
as I have to his biographical, *ſecond-
ſighted* effuſions: for, what ſhall be
ſaid of a perſon, who, after many
printed confeſſions of conſtant kind-
neſs, goes deliberately through an
extenſive track of country, drink-
ing your drink, eating your bread,
repoſing on your bed, and then,
with *premeditated* malignity, dip-

F   ping

ping his goofe-quill in gall, and returning into his own country, merely to fwell her triumph over that, which hath cherifhed him? Is it not, my Lord, (to adopt the nervous language of that Shake-fpeare whom he hath *elucidated* in= to *obfcurity*)*

" As his hand,
Should tear the *mouth* that lifting
food to't?"

I cannot think that, a greater mis-fortune can attend a people, than for thefe fnarlers, (who from the na-ture of their conftitutions and their cloiftered habits of life, ever look on the black fide of the profpect;) to vifit any nation as *literary* travel-

* Alluding to Dr. J—'s edition of Shakefpear.

lers,

lers, fince they travel not with in-
tent to give the world a fair account
of manners and cuftoms, but merely
to exaggerate the bad and fink the
good. This is the natural confequence arifing from the writings of
a Dr. J——, which ought to meet
with the contempt that a falfe reprefentation of a very worthy fet
of people deferves. The length
of my letter frightens me, therefore I will not add a word more
than that

I am, my Lord,

your much obliged fervant.

LETTER VIII.

To Lady Mary B———

Edinburgh, August 18, 1775.

WHEN we returned to Edinburgh, my dear Lady Mary, we made a party to dine at Rosline Castle, a place which hath given its name to one of their pretty plaintive tunes, of which you are such an admirer. We are apt to consider such places as the classic ground of Scotland; which hath certainly produced some pathetic poets, as well as illustrious historians;

rians; and we have as much pleafure in fitting under the bufhes of
Traquair, the birks of Invermay,
or on the banks of the Tweed,
liftening to the fongs of the poets,
as in reading the profounder pages
of Philofophy, or tracing the biographical annals of the *hiftoric* Mufe.

Rofline Caftle is fituated on a little
hillock on the banks of the river
Efk. It appears by the thicknefs of
the walls, and the extent of the foun-
dation, to have been a ftrong place;
and was the feat of a prince of Ork-
ney, who an old woman, — the
Cicerone of the place—affured us,
was the fecond man in the kingdom,
and that his wife was dreffed in velvet;

this

this was all the information *she* could give *us*, and, therefore, all I can give *you*.—The chapel, which lies about 200 yards from the castle, is more modern; and, though our old woman descanted on its antiquity, by the fiddles and other ornaments on the roof, cannot be above 400 years old. The pillars that support it are all different in form, and one of them, which is thought the handsomest, though I cannot tell why, is called the Prince's pillar, or the 'prentice's—our conductress told us a legend of the master's having killed his 'prentice through envy, because he had excelled him in the construction of it. I own I

saw

faw nothing to envy in the beauty of any pillar there; but then it muft be confidered, that perhaps I under-ftand as little of the beauties of architecture, as thofe by whom thefe pillars were planned. There is a vaulted chapel underneath the other, which has a holy-water fount, and other remains of the popifh de-corations; which makes me wonder how it efcaped the rage of refer-mation with fo little damage.—Near this place is a pretty little inn, where we had moft excellent trout and eels juft taken from the river below us:—the poultry too was fuperior to what we generally meet with,

F 4

and

and the civility of the people rendered it one of the moſt agreeable
jaunts I have yet had.—Before I
conclude my letter, (tho' I am
afraid you are already yawning over
it) I muſt preſent you with an elegy,
or a ſong, or a ſomething, which a
gentleman has lately wrote on this
delightful ſpot: it conveys a very
good idea both of the ruinous and
flouriſhing beauties of the place.
You will, perhaps, not value very
highly the production of a Northern
Muſe, nor would you ſcarcely imagine
at times, there was heat enough in
the climate to kindle the enthuſiaſm
of the bard: But I doubt not *you*
will be (as *I* was) of a contrary
opinion,

opinion, when you have perufed the
following ftanzas; and that I may
no longer detain you from them,
I conclude myfelf,

Yours, fincerely.

R O S.

ROSLINE CASTLE.

AT dead of night, the hour, when courts
   In gay fantaſtic pleaſures move,
And haply Mira joins their ſports,
   And hears ſome newer, richer love ;
To ROSLINE's ruins I repair,
   A ſolitary wretch forlorn ;
To mourn, uninterrupted, there,
   My hapleſs love, her hapleſs ſcorn.

No ſound of joy diſturbs my ſtrain,
   No hind is whiſtling on the hill ;
No hunter winding o'er the plain ;
   No maiden ſinging at the rill.
Eſk, murm'ring thro' the duſky pines,
   Reflects the moon's miſt-mantled beam ;
And fancy chills, where'er it ſhines,
   To ſee pale ghoſts obſcurely gleam.

No:

Not fo the night, that in thy halls
   Once, ROSLINE, danc'd in joy along;
Where owls now fcream along thy walls,
   Refounded mirth-infpiring fong:
Where bats now reft their fmutty wings,
   Th' impurpled feaft was wont to flow;
And Beauty danc'd in graceful rings,
   And Princes fat, where nettles grow.

What now avails, how great, how gay;
   How fair, how fine, their matchlefs
     dames!
There, fleeps their undiftinguifh'd clay,
   And even the ftones have loft their names.
And yon gay crowds muft foon expire!
   Unknown, unprais'd, their Fair-one's
     name:
Not fo the charms that verfe infpire,
   Encreafing years encreafe her fame.

                  Oh!

Oh Mira! what is ſtate or wealth?
　　The Great can never love like me;
Wealth adds not days, nor quickens health;
　　Then wiſer thou, come, happy be;
Come, and be mine in this ſweet ſpot,
　　Where Eſk rolls clear his little wave,
We'll live—and Eſk ſhall, in a *cot*,
　　See joys that ROSLINE never gave.

LETTER IX.

To MISS ——————

Tay-Bridge, August 25, 1775.

I Received my dear sister's agreeable favor, just as I was leaving Edinburgh for my northern expedition; which has, hitherto, been fraught sufficiently with adventures to entitle us to the honourable order of Quixotism, and to confer upon your correspondent the dignity of a Lady-Errant. But to let you see I do not complain without reason, I will give you the journal

5   of

of the laſt four days.—Wedneſday, we lay at Mr. Seton's, a very pretty Highland place, three miles from Sterling, made doubly agreeable by the hoſpitality and politeneſs of its owner.—Thurſday, after breakfaſt, we ſet out for Crief, where one of the horſes fell ſick, and we were forced to ſtay.—Friday, proved a day of misfortunes. Indeed, we had ſcarce quitted the houſe when the horſe appeared almoſt too bad to go on. The road was rather diſagreeable, laying between immenſe " cloud-topt" hills, which ſtrike with awe and wonder the aſtoniſhed beholder. But it is in vain to attempt a deſcription, as none can

convey

convey an adequate idea of those
stupendous mountains. They were
not like Dr. J——s hill, *perpendicu-
larly inflated*, but they rather an-
swered the description of a poet not
much less laboriously affected; Sir
Richard Blackmore of rumbling
memory :

" Ridges of high contiguous hills arise,
" Divide the hills, and penetrate the skies."

When we arrived within three miles
of our stage, the horses would not
go any farther; there was no resource, but to unharness and bait
them, while we took up our abode
in a hovel filled with hay; which
place might, I think, justly be
stiled, A place (in the language of
a coun-

a country fign) affording *Entertain-ment for Man and Beaft*. Here we fat an hour and an half; till, being quite frozen with cold, I was obliged to take the fhelter of a little hut, the inhabitants of which made me a fire, and treated me with un-taught good-nature and hofpitality. The fentiments of poor Goldfmith were perfonified, and I *faw* the very fcene he hath fo pleafingly painted in his Traveller. With involuntary ardour, and to the infi-nite furprife of the good people of the cottage, I broke forth into quotation, and applied the Travel-ler's language.

"Bleft

" Bleſt be this ſpot, where chearful gueſts
retire,
To pauſe from toil, and trim their evening
fire;
Blefs'd this abode, where travellers repair,
And every ſtranger finds a ready chair :
Bleſt be theſe feaſts, with ſimple plenty
crown'd,
Where all the ruddy family around,
Laugh at the pranks or jeſts that never fail;
Or ſigh with pity at ſome mournful tale,
Or preſs the baſhful ſtranger to his food,
And learn the luxury of doing good."

But alas ! this Arcadian liberality
is too ſeldom found in houſes
of the genteel and poliſhed part of
the world; for, certainly, benevo-
lence is cemented with our beings,
and we are delighted in obeying the

G   dictates

dictates of nature; till art, that
spoiler of many natural good qualities, makes us assume a look and
behaviour, foreign to our hearts;
for who, my dear sister, chooses to
appear in their own character, where
all around them are in masquerade?
Your true men of the world, those
men, my sister, who pique themselves upon the adoption of fashion-
able maxims, and who move in
the sphere of elevated duplicity,

" Can smile, and smile, and murder while
　　they smile,
And cry, content to that which grieves the
　　heart;
Can wet the cheek with artificial tears,
And frame the face to all occasions:

Such

"Such can deceive more flyly than Ulyffes,
"Such can add colours even to the cameleon,
"Change fhapes with Proteus for advantages,
And fend the murd'rous Machiavel to
    fchool."

But to quit extracts, and proceed—
With all this trouble we could get
but eleven miles this day, and lay
at Hamilrow, a place, where, from
its fituation and appearance, it is
impoffible to harbour any thing but
gloomy ideas. And, were an En-
glifhman or woman to lodge here
in the bleak black month of No-
vember, the confequences might be
fatal. Even I, (who you know,
have none of the faturnine difpo-
fition of my country) could not

help declaring, I would not live there one week to be miftrefs of all the furrounding hills : for, be it known, the eye can difcover nothing *but* thofe hills. This morning, we left the dreary place to meet with worfe mifadventures than before. We had not proceeded a mile when the horfes run back, inftead of afcending a hill, and broke the pole, which luckily hindered the chaife from running back. We got out, and walked up; but neither ill or good ufage could prevail on *them* to follow : we now found their only difeafe was being reftive : With a great deal of trouble they were perfuaded to

go

go two miles farther; when, on the appearance of *another* hill, they performed the fame trick, with fome confiderable additions; for they would not move a foot. What was to be done? there were no horfes at the place we had left, and it was twelve miles to Taybridge, where if we had fent, it was very unlikely we fhould be better fupplied, there being no poft-horfes kept on the Highland roads. In this terrible dilemma—chance, a goddefs which is worfhipped by not a few, ftood our friend, and fent us help. She did not appear in the form of an Oroondates, mounted on a milk-white palfrey, fhining

in burnished armour, and a helmet
waving with feathers, like the toasts
of Britain: no, she came to us in
a much more desirable shape than
all the knights of Chivalry, from
Amadis de Gaul, to the famous
knight of La Manca. We beheld
her goddesship in the similitude of
a return post-chaise, whose driver
was, by the all attracting and charming
power of gold, prevailed on to put
his horses before ours, by which
means, we got safe to Tay-bridge.
Till we came to Sterling, we had
passed our journey without any
trouble, but who had a right to expect, it would continue? It was
emblematic of our great journey

ney through life, where all muſt
meet with their *black*, as well as
white days, but we ſhould ſatisfy
ourſelves with conſidering,

" Tis not for *nothing* that we life purſue;
It pays our hopes with ſomething ſtill that's
    new :
Each day's a miſtreſs unenjoy'd before,
Like *travellers*, we're pleas'd with *ſeeing*
    more."
Bravo! Mr. Dryden.

Adieu, my dear ſiſter, you ſhall
ſoon hear from me ___, if I
_____
_____
_____.

_____
_____
G 4

LETTER X.

To Lady Mary B————

Taymouth, August 18, 1775.

AFTER innumerable perils and dangers, here I am, my dear Lady Mary, once more lodged in safety in an *enchanting* castle. Take notice, I did not say an *enchanted* one, though could fairy tales now gain credit, this might well pass for one of their palaces; but before I give you a description of it, I must inform you, that, for some days past, I have been traveling

ling through places fo gloomy, that
was I to attempt to defcribe them,
it would give you the vapours for
this month to come : But after we
came within fome miles of·this place
and began to defcend into the vale,
the country wore a moft pleafing appearance; the contraft being fo ftrik-
ingly beautiful, from thofe truly barren rocks, to this cultivated valley,
which continues to encreafe in beauty till you arrive at Taymouth, the
feat of Lord Breadalbane. This
place, is faid to carry the prize
from all others in the Highlands,
and well does it deferve to do fo.
For this favoured fpot feems to
enjoy every benefit of the boafted
South.

South. Nature having poured out her bleffings with the hand of profufion; every thing appears to grow with the greateft luxuriance: And the tafte and fpirit of his Lordfhip cannot be too much admired. Nature is affifted by art, juft enough to add to, not rob her of, her beauties; which laft is in general the fault of moft modern improvers. How few men of property practife the precepts of Mr. Pope,

"To build, to plant, whatever you intend,
To rear the column, or the arch to bend;
To fwell the terrace, or to fink the grot,
In all, let Nature never be forgot:

But

But treat the Goddefs like a modeft Fair,
Nor over-drefs, nor leave her wholly bare;
Let not each beauty ev'ry-where be fpy'd,
Where half the fkill is decently to hide.
He gains all points who pleafing'y con-
      founds,
Surprizes, varies, and conceals the bounds."

Taymouth lies in a fertile v
bounded on each fide by mountains
planted with trees and
The policy furrounds the
which ftands in the park, a
very good one, ftocked
deer, which are rarities i
their's being the red
a magnificent walk
large trees, forming a
which may, from its thick

bid defiance to Sol's moſt refulgent
beams. The walk on the banks of
the Tay is fifty feet wide, and two
and twenty hundred yards long; not
that I meaſured it, but ſo ſaid my
informer. It is to be continued as
far as the meeting of the two rivers,
the Tay and the Lion; which will
make it as long again as it now is;
and it may then be ſaid to ſtand
unrivalled in this country. We
will now, if you are not tired, take
a tour over the wooden bridge that
is thrown acroſs the Tay, and is
two hundred feet long, and aſcend
the oppoſite hill to the white ſeat,
where you have a magnificent and
extenſive view of the rich meadows,

the

the various windings of the river, the beginning of the Lough Tay, which has a very pretty island upon it, with the ruins of a priory, founded by Alexander the first, in 1122; in which were deposited the remains of his Queen Sybilla, natural daughter to Henry the First. It was founded by Alexander, that the monks might pray for the repose of his soul, and that of his queen. What absurdity in the Romish religion, to imagine that any set of men, sinners like ourselves, could have power to pray us out of purgatory!—Here is a very pretty edifice called The Temple of Venus, in which is a statue

6 of

of the laughter-loving Dame. You have from it a fine view. There is another to Apollo, and one to Boreas, and many more of the fabulous deities, to which his Lordship has raised temples; from all of which you have fine prospects. The castle is large, and there are many of the pictures of the famous Jansen, a scholar of Rubens, the Vandyk of this country: of whose performances they are extremely fond; the genealogical picture of this family done by *him*, is esteemed a curiosity. I think it a very good method to hand down pedigrees by making the first of the family the trunk, and all his progeny the branches.

branches. I know you love long
letters, but by the time you have
got to the end of this, you will
have little reafon to complain. I
have but juft room in my paper
to tell my dear Lady Mary,

I am,

her much obliged friend, &c.

LET-

LETTER XI.

To the EARL of C————

Dunkeld, August 30, 1775.

EVER since I had the pleasure of writing to your Lordship from Sterling, I met with a series of disagreeable adventures, till I arrived at Taymouth castle, the seat of Lord Breadalbane, which we left Tuesday after dinner; and pursued our way for Dunkeld. The road is charming all the way; but being late when I arrived, hindered me

from

from enjoying beſt part of the proſpect it afforded.

" The glimmering landſcape faded on the
ſight."

Wedneſday we croſſed the river
and landed in the Duke of Athol's
garden: it is ſituated on the banks
of the Tay, and you have from
the walks ſome fine wild views;
there is a number of trees
that thrive very well. In the garden is the ruin of the cathedral, a
noble and ſtately edifice, as may be
ſeen from the pillars ſtill ſtanding,
round which, the claſping ivy
creeps: Theſe conſecrated ruins always fill me with melancholy re-

H   flections,

flections, for which that levelling reformer Knox, has given occasion enough in this country; all but one (as observed in a former letter;)* are mouldering in ruins.

" Around, you see, wild rugged heaps of
  stone,
" Where pillars once of Parian marble
  shone :
" Yet conscious what, those ruins were of
  old,
" Who dares unmov'd, the mossy walls be-
  hold ?
" I tremble at the Deity's abode,
" And own the powerful presence of the
  God."

* See Letter the VIIth.

One

One cannot, my Lord, behold such venerable reliques without a religious awe; and poetry is frequently called in to aid contemplation. The ruins of an abby, a cathedral, or a castle, are, methinks, more memento's of our own mortality No wonder, therefore, that our most eminent writers have pathetically described those universal depredations of time and chance, which happen to all men. The aptness of the following verses, to the solemnity of my subject, struck me; and they are too apropos to the occasion, and too admirable in themselves, to need an excuse for inserting

H 2   i.

ing them fo many miles to your
Lordfhip.

What does not fade! The Tower that long
    had ftood
The crufh of thunder, and the warring
    winds,
Shook by the flow, but fure deftroyer Time,
Now hangs in doubtful ruins o'er its bafe,
And flinty pyramids, and walls of brafs,
Defcend ; the Babylonian fpires are funk ;
Achaia, Rome, and Egypt moulder down,
Time fhakes the ftable tyranny of thrones,
And tottering empires rufh by their own
    weight.
This huge rotundity we tread, grows old,
And all thofe worlds that roll around the
    fun,
The fun himfelf fhall die; and antient
    night
Again involve the defolate abyfs:

                        Till

Till the great Father, through the lifelefs
    gloom,
Extend his arm to light another world,
And bid new planets roll by other laws;
For through the regions of unbounded
    fpace,
Where unconfin'd Omnipotence has rcom,
Being, in various fyftems fluctuates ftill
Between creation and abhorred decay :
It ever did, perhaps and ever will
New worlds are ftill emerging from the
    deep,
The old defcending, in their turns to rife.

But to quit philofophical reflections, and purfue our remarks on
the pleafure grounds of the Duke
of Athol.—In the walk that is by
the river, is a grotto ornamented
in an uncommon way; it is built

of large coarfe ftones, on each
of which are written verfes on various fubjects from moft of the
Englifh poets. This little retire-
ment may be faid to afford food for
the mind; there are fome by the
late Duke himfelf, one of which
I tranfcribed with my pencil, and
I here fend you a copy :

" Whilft refting on this rural feat,
" In this one hour of fweet retreat,
" Oh! may my heart with thanks o'er-
  flow,
" For all the good Heaven *did* beftow,
" For every blefling—ftill poffefs'd,
" Oh render thanks, my grateful breaft.
" May they, to whom this feat is lent,
" With every good poffefs content;
     " Thank-

" Thankful to God for all that's given,
" Tread virtue's path, the path to heaven.

　　　　　　　D— A—d."

Thefe lines though paffing well for a nobleman, who writes only for diverfion, are by no means elegant or correct enough for a *profeffed* poet. It may feem fomewhat fpiteful therefore to defire your Lordfhip will read after them a defcription of a fimilar fpot by one of the moft agreeable writers on fubjects of fimplicity, that ever adorned the court of Pan or Silvanus.—Yet, I could have wifhed the Duke had found a place for the fubfequent truly rural, and enchanting ftanzas.

H 4　　　　　　　Your

Your Lordſhip will ſee, they derive
additional beauty by the air of antiquity in ſpelling the words, ex-
cluſive of a ruſticity perfectly venerable in the ſentiment.

O you that bathe in courtly bliſſe,
   Or toyle in Fortune's giddy ſphere;
Do not too raſhly deem amyſſe
   Of him that bides contented here.

Nor yet diſdeigne the ruſſet ſtoale,
   Which o'er each carleſs lymb he flings;
Nor yet deryde the beechen bowle,
   In which he quaffs the lympid ſprings.

Forgive him, if at eve, or dawn
   Devoide of worldlye caſh he ſtray;
Or all beſide ſome flowerye lawn,
   He waſte his inoffenſive daye.

On

On the other side of this river is
a pretty romantic walk that leads
to the hermitage: on the rock at
the end of it is a neat pavillion,
whose windows are formed or painted glafs, through which you fee the
river falling from a furprising height
into the horrid gulph beneath, with
a moft terrifying noife; and that
which adds greatly to the formi-
dable grandeur of the fcene is, that
by looking through that part of the
window which is red, it appears to
be fheets of liquid fire rolling down
the rock like the lava of mount
Etna. My ideas were fo lively in
picturing fuch images of horror
that I was obliged to turn it

indulg

indulging them, or from farther contemplating the scene.——We are just going to set out for Blair, and the summons of the postilion obliges me abruptly to conclude myself,

Your Lordship's

moft obliged humble fervant.

LET-

LETTER XII.

To LADY MARY B————

Dalvey, September 6, 1775.

BY the date of this, my dear Lady Mary, you will fee I have got to the end of my journey. But I will, as you defire, continue the journal of the laft four days before I arrived at this place—Wednefday, we left Dunkeld and fet out for Blair. The road between thofe two places is one of the moft agreeable I ever travelled, being all the way along the banks of the river

river Tay, which prefents at one
view corn fields, woods of natural
oaks, plantations of fir trees; and
in the back ground, immenfe rocks,
whofe rugged fides form a moft
ftriking and beautiful contraft to
the pleafing vale below. I think
nothing in nature can lull our tur-
bulent paffions, and give to the
mind that fweet ferenity fo truly
defireable, and fo feldom found,
as fuch a profpect in the delici-
oufly-pacific calm of a fummer
evening. Such was the effect I
found from it; for my fentiments
always flow from my feelings—
Thurfday we took a view of Blair,
a feat of the Duke of Athol's: the
house

house is now modernized, but once it was fortified, and held a siege against the rebels in 1746. Indeed, I believe, there are few castles in the Highlands, which before the Union, have not withstood an attack, either from their neighbours or some more distant invader, as it was their great delight to harrass and distress one another. Near the house is a fine walk of trees, which encloses a glen, and a cascade that falls from a great height; but I do not think it half so desireable a place to live in as Dunkeld. We now set out to pursue our journey, and made the first stage very well; but it was not destined, that we

should

should reach our wished-for haven, without a few of those tremendous adventures, that give an air of the wonderful, in the recital of modern travels, in the recounting which, there is a sort of biographical licence allowed, or at least taken, of which, however, I promise not to avail myself, as I have not a pen for *embellishing*: I'll content myself in recounting facts, as they happened. We had got a few miles from our last stage when, on the appearance of a very high hill, opposite Loch Geary, the horses run the chaise close to the edge of the precipice. Happily, we were out of it, or I think we should soon have

been

been with our anceſtors in the ſhades below: they broke the pole in this barren place, the very worſt ſpot it could have happened in. We were forced to ſit an hour and a half, whilſt the carriage was dragged up the hill by the poſt-boy, with the aſſiſtance of one old man and three old women, they being all the human creatures this diſmal place afforded. There were now eight miles to go with a broken pole, which took up another hour in the mending, but by nine o'clock at night, we arrived in ſafety—Friday morning we ſet out again, when on the ſight of a little hill, within four miles of Pit-main, thoſe villainous horſes performed

formed their accustomed trick, and broke the pole in a *second* place so bad, that we were obliged to walk those four miles, and have a new pole before we could pursue our ill-fated journey: there was no resource but patience — Saturday morning, left Pitmain, dined at Avely Moor, and arrived at tea at Sir James Grant's at Castle Grant—Left it on Sunday morning, and concluded all my adventures for the present by getting to Dalvey at dinner—Don't you give me joy—for fond as I am of travelling, I feel myself very happy in the idea of resting for some time. You must now write a great deal to me without expecting much

in

in return, as the *still* life I am like-
ly to lead for some time will produce little worth recounting.

I am,

my dear Lady Mary's

sincere friend.

I   LET-

LETTER XIII.

To Miss ————

Dalvey, September 16, 1775.

YOU afk me, my dear Sifter, for a defcription of this place. Inclination and obedience go hand in hand in every requeft you can poffibly make. Take then the following general fketches—The houfe has nothing worthy remark but its fituation, which is enchanting, being built on an afcent, which in England, might well be ftiled a hill. The gardens are much below it; at

2 the

the bottom of which runs a beautiful little river over a pebbley bed. I call it little at this time, but they tell me, in the winter after great rains, it becomes a flood. I am not willing to believe that an object at present so inoffensive, can ever become one of terror and affright. Appearances, however, are not to be trusted; since it is but too usual to see the most amiable-seeming objects, turn upon a nearer view, to the most alarming and dangerous;

"All are not what they seem."

However, I hope not to run here late enough in the autumn to see this tranquil stream become a turbid torrent. At the same time I muſt acquaint you that the account the people of the country give me of it, anſwers preciſely to that deſcription of an over-bearing flood mentioned in Homer—The woman's Homer, you may be ſure, is, Mr. Pope's tranſlation:

" Thus from high *hills*, the torrents ſwift
    and ſtrong,
Deluge whole fields, and ſweep the trees
    along."

From the windows you have a fine view of the ſea, and of the town and the harbour of Findorn: and behind that, the hills of Roſsſhire riſe to view in magnificent arrangement;

ment; while around, you are prefented with a fine plain rich in corn,
abounding with wood, and inter-
fperfed with gentlemen's feats. They
tell you this county has fix weeks
longer fummer than any other in
Scotland: I really believe it, for,
never did I experience fuch fine
weather: They are bleft with an ho-
rizon of the brighteft azure, without a cloud. Here are likewife fome
of the prettieft walks, along the
winding of the Bourn; and the beautiful and ferene ftillnefs of the even-
ings here, after a fine day, is beyond
expreffion delightful: 'tis altogether the Elyfium of Caledonia; and,
whatever ill-natured pens may fay

I 3   to

to the contrary, is not inferior to
the moſt cultivated village in England. Never were ſcenes, or objects, more ſuited to ſerene contemplation.

" Here let me lie, where infant flow'rets blow,
Where ſweeteſt verdure paints the ground
      below;
Where the ſhrill warblers charm the ſolemn
      ſhade,
And zephyrs pant along the cooler glade;
Where ſhakes the bullruſh by a river-ſide,
While the gay ſun-beams ſparkle on the
      tide.
Oh! for ſome grot whoſe ruſtic ſides de-
      clare,
Eaſe, and not ſplendour, was the builder's
      care:
Where happy ſilence lulls the quiet ſoul,
And makes it calm as ſummer waters roll.

Here

Here let me learn to check each growing ill,
And bring to reason disobedient will;
To watch this incoherent breast, and find,
What favourite passions rule the giddy
  mind.
Here no reproaches grate the wounded ear,
We see delighted, and transported hear,
While the glad warblers wanton round the
  trees,
And the still waters catch the dying breeze.
Come, every thought which Virtue gave to
  please !
Come, smiling Health, with thy companion
  Ease :
Let these, and all that Virtue's self attend;
Bless the still hour of Sister and of Friend,
Peace to my foes, if any such there be,
And gracious Heaven give kind repose to
  me."

Thus, my dear, you see when I
am become bankrupt, and have ex-
hausted my little stock of sentiment,
remark, or description, I draw upon
the poets, for a fresh, and indeed,
a far richer supply, whenever I re-
collect in their writings any pas-
sages a-propos to the subject in
hand. In short, with respect to
this spot, nothing is wanting but
an Amintas, to make me imagine myself in Arcadia. Indeed, I
think you say something on that
subject in your last. — Remember,
my dear sister, my province is
to make *remarks* not *conquests*. I

am

am juſt going to take a ſolitary ramble.

Adieu.

Ever yours, &c. &c.

LET-

LETTER XIII.

To the EARL *of* C————

Dalvey, September 22, 1775.

I Have at laft croffed the Highlands in fafety, and I find myfelf fituated once more in a flat
country, with the hills which furrounded us before, thrown behind
us.

Murray, is a rich plain, cultivated, even to a delicacy of luxuriance; efpecially in point of corn,
which may rival the boafted production

duction of the Englifh foil, even in the center of Surry.

This houfe is venerable from its antiquity, and hath juft that monumental moffinefs, and antedeluvian air about it, which would ftrongly recommend it to our virtuofc's in architecture. It is decorated, or rather fortified with turrets, from whence the original proprietors were accuftomed to fhoot their arrows, and fire their mufquets, in order to annoy their invaders. Indeed, all the caftles of this country are built for defence; which precaution was but too neceffary in times of civil commotions amongft themfelves;

and

and it appears that they were always altercating; so that nothing but arms, and structures almost impregnable, could render either their persons or their property in any degree secure : especially as those who maintained the contest against them were more powerful. Let it be observed too, that their rapacious neighbours took every possible advantage of their weakness, or want of force; and, as is the common practice of war, to have the *power* to distress, and the inclination to *use* that power, was exactly one and the same thing. This, however, will cease to surprise, when we consider that every chieftain was absolute folute monarch, and fovereign difpofer of his own particular clan; that he ftyled himfelf patron and proprietor of all his tenants, whofe wills, purfuits, and paffions he held in vaffalage. By virtue of this authority, however originally obtained, or with whatever tyranny carried on, thefe chieftains, could with all the fupremacy of an oriental potentate, lead forth their flaves to battle; and that, without any nice regard to the juftice of the caufe, or to the propriety of the bloody engagement. The mandate of the chieftain was the univerfal law as far as his own *chieftaincy* extended, and he could direct the warrior to

twang

twang his bow, or difcharge his muf-
quet, upon any occafion, without
affigning any equable reafon for fo
doing: Hence, it very frequently
happened, that, a chieftain would involve his flavifh fubjects in the ca-
lamities of public conteft, to gratify his private ambition, his envy,
or his avarice. Such, in fact, was
the general practice all over this
country, till the union with England regulated the power, and put
an end to the inhofpitable bicker-
ings of thefe petty princes, and
chieftains: Add to which, the many
wife acts fince paffed, have given a
proper proportion of liberty to the
commonalty. Induftry, civiliza-
tion,

tion, and plenty, are the natural
consequence of such political, public measures: Notwithstanding this,
it was a good while before either
the higher or lower degrees of the
Scots, could be brought to consider
the union of the kingdoms as either
constitutional or safe any. Time,
however, with its reconciling power,
hath rubbed off these prejudices;
and I dare say there are none of
either rank, who do not rejoice at
the friendship which subsists between
the two countries. Near this place,
is Forres in the moor, near which
Shakespeare hath placed the last
interview of Macbeth, and the way-
ward sisters. I have travelled over
the

the fpot thus folemnized by the
monarch of the Britifh drama, pure-
ly for the intellectual pleafure of
treading on claffic ground; but fince
the Witch Act has been repealed, I
believe the very idea of enchantment
and preter-natural appearances, is
almoft extinct, even in this, once
fuperftitious country: at leaft I
can affure your Lordfhip, I met,
in *my* rambles acrofs this charmed
foil, no fine promifes from either
male or female conjurors. — You
have from this moor a fine view
of Rofsfhire, and the noble entrance
into the bay of Cromartie, between
two lofty hills; forming a beautiful and picturefque piece of fcenery.

On

'On the north, is KINLOSS Abby, a fine ruin, and the place where the bones of many of their Scotch kings are mixed with their parent duſt. Forres is a very pretty town; at the weſt end of which, are the wretched remains of Macbeth's caſtle. If I ſhould meet with any thing while I am here, worth troubling you to read, your Lordſhip ſhall hear again from

> your moſt obedient ſervant.

K   L E T-

LETTER XIV.

To LADY MARY B————

Dalvey, October 4, 1775.

I am to thank my dear Lady Mary for her very entertaining letter; and I think, I cannot do so more to the purpose, than by fulfilling her commands; and, as well as I am able, give her some description of the customs and manners of this people. The Highland ladies are, as with us, some very pretty, others not: They have strong passions; among which are, pride of

ancestry,

anceftry, and a fcrupulous care
not to degenerate by mixing with
plebeian blood. There are many
ladies here, who would rather
prefer marrying a *Chieftain*, and
live fecluded from the world o
fix hundred a year, than join themfelves to a Lowlander, whofe progenitors were born a few hundred
years later, with treble that fum.
I don't think the *gentlemen* are fuch
dupes to this foible; for, having
moft of them travelled, they know
the worth of gold, and prize it accordingly; by confequence, would
have no objection to a rich citizen's
daughter with a plumb. It was not
long fince a gentleman of a fecond

try married in London, and brought down here a broker's daughter, who gives herself more airs than a Duchess. This family-pride excepted, they are a very agreeable set of people, good-natured, sensible, and polite: they love dancing to excess, and are the best country-dancers I ever saw, and *keep it up* (as the phrase is) for hours together, with a life, vivacity and spirit, of which you can have no conception. In many houses, they still retain the ancient custom of the pipers playing all the time the company are at dinner, on his *horrid bagpipes*; this is to *me* more dreadful, than the grunting of pigs, the screaming

of

of owls, and the fqualling of cats. All thefe creatures in a concert would be to my ears pleafing, compared to that difcordant inftrument to which I have a natural antipathy. I was laft Sunday, for the firft time, at a Highland kirk, or church; and fuch a ftrange performance as the lower fort of women make would amaze you. The married ones wear a handkerchief croffed over their heads, with the ends pinned under their chin; the third flying behind; the young ones wear nothing but a ribband in their hair; the other parts of their drefs are like thofe of the common people with us; only over all, the wear a plaid, which reaches to their feet, and is wrapped over their head, so that nothing is left to be seen but their noses——The poorest sort of all, who cannot afford a plaid, rather than not be ornamented, walk forth arrayed in their blankets; so that when all are assembled in this strange fashion they really have just the appearance of a set of lunaticks. All here sing psalms; those who are fortunate enough to have a voice, and those that are not so fortunate, which sounds are very far from exciting the spirit of devotion. It surprises me, that I have seldom seen a *pretty* girl among the lower class, which

5 is

is so frequent here than: The only
reason in my o
for it is, that fe
much on delicacy;
laborious part which
take in this country wh
accounts for their bein
disagreeable: so that d
little temptation for a
country to form amour, or h
his inclination to gallantry.
there is still a stronger thin
their plainness to deter him,
in this case; for if
with child, both of them are o
to do *public penance*, and the
gyman reads them a lecture of
proof *before the whole*

This mode of chaſtiſement appears
to me very well calculated to keep
them honeſt, as the ſhame attending the puniſhment will hinder the
committing the crime, by which it
is incurred. There is hardly ever
ſuch a thing heard of, as a Highland highway robber; their roads
are not, like ours, infeſted by thoſe
peſts to ſociety. Your purſe and
your perſon are here equally ſecure;
nor do their news-papers, like
ours, ſhock humanity every month
with an account of five or ſix and
twenty poor wretches condemned to
an ignominious death, the conſe-
quence of Engliſh voluptuouſneſs.
Their laws too are wiſely calculated
for

for the good of the community in
general, and their church is under
most excellent regulations; their liv-
ings are from forty pounds a year
to one hundred and fifty, with a
decent house and some land: not, as
with us, a vicar, with eight hundred or a thousand a year, will give
thirty pounds to a poor curate t
do the duty of three par
maintain a wife and t
but here, the cler
equality; one ma
three or four *fi*   no
they allowed a cur e, but in c
of real sickness. I   v
you all the infor
of their *laws* and

I muſt own before I came to Scotland, I had, from wrong repreſentations, conceived a very different character than what they deſerve. I ſincerely wiſh I had a pen equal to the taſk of juſtifying them and their country from thoſe illiberal aſperſions under which they have too long laboured, from a ſet of men, whoſe prejudices are ſuch, that they think wiſdom and worth confined to one ſpot only, and that ſpot without doubt, they think *their own.* May my breaſt never harbour ſuch contracted ſentiments, as I am convinced, that virtue is the growth of every clime!

" Go

" Go ſearch it there, where to be born and
     die,
Of rich and poor, make all the hiſtory;
Enough that virtue fill'd the ſpace between,
Prov'd by the *ends* of being, to have been :
Virtue may chooſe the *high* or *low* degree,
'Tis juſt alike to virtue and to me :
Dwell in a monk or light upon a king,
She's ſtill the ſame belov'd, contented
     thing."

And no country, my dear Lady
Mary, has produced men, more capable of making a ſhining figure
than *Scotland*; as indeed our Senate,
our Army, and our Courts, both of
juſtice and politeneſs can witneſs.
My paper being pretty well filled,
              I am

I am compelled to conclude myfelf, fooner than I could wifh,

your Ladyfhip's

moft obliged friend

and obedient fervant.

LETTER X⸺

To the EARL *of* C⸺

Dalvey, October 2⸺, 1⸺

YOU complain, my ⸺ ⸺
my long filence—I ⸺
beft excufe in the world ⸺
writing; the having not ⸺
taining to fay. A few ⸺ys fi⸺
I was on a party to F⸺ ⸺
it is a ftrong Fortre⸺, ⸺
been built fince Forty-five ⸺s ⸺
fenal for arms: there ⸺
regiment of foot ⸺ ⸺
which are very har⸺ ⸺

some very good ftreets; the armoury
is prettily difpofed, but I never can
conceive much pleafure in behold-
ing fo many inftruments of deftruc-
tion to my fellow-creatures. It
happened to be rough weather,
which gave us a noble and beautiful, and I might add, fublime
profpect of the fea, the waves dafh-
ing againft the rocks half way the
battlements; and as I am greatly
attached to fuch profpects, I was
highly entertained. In our return
we took a view of Cawder Caftle,
a place well known in hiftory for
giving the fecond title to Macbeth:
the old part of the building, is a
fquare tower, in which, they fhew

you

you an old timber bedftead, the fame, they fay, in which Dunca. was murdered. Murdered, my Lord, to place a fhort-lived crown on the head of the ambitious Thane. But if, as the hiftorians fay, that horrid deed was perpetrated at Macbeth's caftle at Invernefs, it is very unlikely, the bed fhould be removed here. People that travel however, muft often depend on the ignorant for information; and have need of a plentiful proportion of faith. I clambered over a quantity of tottering ftone ftairs, every ftep threatening the downfal of unwary ftrangers; even to the top, from whence you have a g...

view of the adjacent country. The woods of Cawder have a great many fine large oak trees, broom, alders, &c. &c. and below, you fee a torrent of water roaring over a bed of rocky ftones, in colour as black as Acheron, and appearing to look as if it was impregnated with all its deadly qualities. The larger part of the building is modern, with a drawbridge; but it is, altogether gloomy and tremendous.

I fhall very foon leave this country for England; and as I fhall return the coaft road to Edinburgh, if I meet in my way any thing

thing interesting, you may, as usual
expect to hear from,

my Lord,

your most obliged,

and very obedient servant.

L   L E T-

LETTER XVI.

To LADY MARY B——————

Bamff, October 25, 1775.

YOU will find, my dear friend, by this, that, like birds of paffage, we are on our flight to our winter habitation ; nor was it before there was occafion, for we left Dalvey three days fince, and have had nothing but hail and rain all the way to this place ; which has made the air intenfely cold, and we very defirous to fmell the fmoak of London, and enjoy the jovial converfe

of

of my agreeable friends. The first
day we dined at L___in, a good
town, but from the stillness of the
streets, I believe, has but little trade.
I went to see the ruins of the Cathedral, it has been both a magnificent and beautiful pile of building.
There are two towers still standing;
but the centre and spire are ruins,
and with the monuments of the en-
nobled dead, form one undistin-
guished heap. Boethius says, that
Duncan, murdered by Macbeth, is
buried here, but there is no monument remaining to gratify the curious. I deplored the Gothic out-
rage, which levelled so fine a structure. We lay at Gordon castle

L 2

large houfe, the feat of the Duke
of Gordon. It has fome good,
well-grown woods round it; but is
far from being built in a defireable
fituation, lying in a low fwampy
bottom. We left it early in the
morning, and had a difagreeable
day's travelling, which afforded
nothing worth relating. The next
morning we breakfafted at Cullen,
and went to take a view of Cullen-
houfe, the feat of the Earl of Finlater.
It is fituated at the edge of a very
deep glen, full of large trees, laid
out in pretty walks, which, being
fheltered from the fea winds, are in
a very profperous ftate: Over the
entrance is a magnificent arch fixty

3   feet

feet high, and eighty-two in width: The houſe is large but irregularly built. There are ſome very good pictures here, but the moſt remark-able are, a full length of James the Sixth, by Mytens, redeemed from the fury of the mob, at the time of the Revolution, by the Earl of Fin-later, at that time Chancellor; a portrait of James Duke of Hamil-ton beheaded in 1649; a half length of his brother, killed at the battle of Worceſter, both by Vandyk; William Duke of Hamilton, Pre-ſident of the Revolution Parliam. by Kneller; Lord Banff, aged ninety, with a long, white, fur beard. His Lordſhip, at that age, in-curred the reſentment of the church for his gallantries; they certainly did the poor old gentleman great injuſtice, as I think, in this northern climate, *Love*, muſt have loſt its power before that time of life. Here is a beautiful picture of the unfortunate Mary Stuart, drawn in a tight black dreſs, and about her ·neck a ruff, part of her hair turned grey, which is a proof to me, of the juſtice of the remark, that *care*, will have that effect without the concurrence of time. We got to Bamff to dinner, and having ſome time on my hands, I ſet down to let

my

my dear Lady Mary know, that she may soon expect to see me in London; 'till which happy period,

I am,

her most obliged friend.

LETTER XVII.

To the EARL *of* C————

Bamff, *October* 25, 1775.

THIS town, my Lord, is plea-
santly situated on the side of
a hill, has some very good streets
and a handsome town-house. The
Earl of Finlater has got a very
pretty one, seated on an eminence
near the town, and around it some
pretty plantations of trees and
shrubs. It commands a fine and
pleasant prospect. In one of the
apart-

apartments, is a picture of Jame-
fon, done by himfelf, fitting in his
painting room, dreffed like Rubens,
with his hat on, and his pallet in
his hand; on the walls are repre-
fented the picture of Charles the
Firft and his Queen, a head of his
own wife, two fea views, Perfeus
and Andromeda, all the produc-
tions of his pencil. You will per-
ceive, my Lord, by what I have
juft wrote, that, I am not of Dr.
J——'s opinion, who, when he
paffed through this place, thought
there was nothing worthy remark,
though he found fubjects for ill-
natured fatire, as the following is
his account of it, on which I have
taken

taken the liberty to make some strictures:

Speaking of this place (Banff) after describing the houses as miferable huts, he says, " that the " art of joining squares of glass with " lead, is either little used or totally " forgotten here, as the frames of " all their windows are wood;" I would ask, which has the best effect in the appearance of a house, wood frames, or those cemented with lead ? Undoubtedly the first, as it is a more modern invention, and univerfally practifed through England, which, surely he had forgot, and had I not myself, escaped without feeling

feeling such an effect, I should be
apt to imagine the Tweed was pof
fefsed of the qualities of Lethe,
and that a draught of it had the
power to make one forget all that
we had feen before. He regre
that the neceffity of ventilating human habitations had not been four
out among our northern neighbours, or at leaft not practifed, and
thinks, a ftranger may be forgiv-
en, if, he allows himfelf to wifh for
frefher air. In anfwer to this,
I muft, in common ir
I never found my felf in
in Scotland, which could give
leaft reafon, excufe me in
fuch a wifh. I cannot h

6

ing (in which I dare fay the major part of his readers will join me) that, he has raked his remarks from the very loweſt dregs of the people, with whom, I ſhould be ſorry, to ſuppoſe he kept *company*. Yet I am certain he could meet with none of the inconveniencies of which he complains, in any thing or any *where*, a degree above a Highland hut—Nay more, was he to travel through Cornwall, or any of the remoter parts of England, it would be found, that, if he meant to deſcribe poverty and ignorance in the lower claſs of people, there was no neceſſity to have taken a journey as far as Scotland for that purpoſe : but, indeed,

deed, he feems confcious (to fpeak in his own words) that, " the di-
" minutivenefs of his obfervations
" will lay him open to cenfure, and
" take from the dignity of writing."
The event of his publication has confirmed his fear, as all who read that ftrange medley regret, that, a man, who has juftly acquired great literary merit by his other produc-tions, fhould fail fo much in this— Pity for that fame, fo dear to au-thors, he had not contented himfelf with *writing Ramblers*, inftead of *taking* a *ramble*; he either was guid-ed in his defcriptions by unjuft par-tiality, which ought not to be the cafe with any writer; or he was

totally

totally unfit for the task he undertook. Let either, or both be the
case, he has greatly exposed himself
in the attempt; but in truth, where
is the need to censure a man who
condemns himself? and this he pal-
pably does in the concluding lines
of his *Tour*, " having passed my
" time almost wholly in cities,"
says he, " I may have been sur-
" prised by modes of life, and ap-
" pearances of nature, that are fa-
" miliar to men of wider survey,
" and more varied conversation:
" Novelty and ignorance must al-
" ways be reciprocal, and I can-
" not but be conscious that my
" thoughts on national manners
" are

" are the thoughts of one who hath
" feen but little." I perfectly
agree with him in the truth con-
tained in every line of the above
quotation; and I am fenfible, if, on
my return to England, I deliver my
opinions, as freely as I have written
them to your Lordfhip, I fhall lay
myfelf open to criticifm; but I fhall
not fear it, as nothing but juftice
for the oppreft, could have obliged
me to have fpoken my fentiments
on Dr. J———'s hiftorical *Ramble*;
and, for that, I have, though a
woman, fortitude enough to fland
any attack from the pens of *fuch*
critics, in the defence of *our mountainous neighbours.*

I am

I am juft returned from feeing
Duff-houfe, the feat of Lord Fife.
It is a little way from this town;
is a vaft pile of building, with a
fquare tower at each end; the front
is fine, and richly ornamented with
carving; but it looks melancholy,
as if regretting its having no wings;
I don't mean for the fame reafon
the late Earl of C———d did, that
it might fly away, for I really do
not know where it could find a
more pleafant fpot to fix in; but
in its prefent fituation it makes me
think of a fine ftatue without
arms; the rooms are not fo large
as the outfide of the building leads
you to imagine. In the apartments

are

are the pictures of Frances Duchess
of Richmond, a full length, in
black, with a little picture at her
breast, done in 1633 by Vandyke;
some fine heads of Charles the first,
and of his Queen; a head of one
of the family of Duff, with short
grey hair, by Alexander of Corsen-
day. I saw here a number of fine
green-house plants, growing with
the greatest luxuriance, exposed to
the open air; and some myrtles,
that appeared to me five feet high,
which is, in my opinion, a strong
proof that it is nothing but pre-
judice which can make us suppose
any reason why, with proper care,
the plants of all countries may not

M   thrive

thrive here as well as in England. The Scotch for some ages past have been infensible of what degree of improvement their country was capable; but they have now opened their eyes to conviction, and I dare say a hundred years hence, our posterity shall behold them with a spirit of emulation making large strides to equal us; and this once naked country become a towering forest. Near the house is a beautiful shrubbery, with a walk two miles long, the river rolling beneath, and on the opposite side, some very noble rocks make it a sweetly-pleasing scene.

3

I am

I am fure you will be frightened at the length of my letter, but it will afford you fome comfort when I tell you it will be the laft time you will hear from me, as I fhall foon have the pleafure of feeing you in Old England, and tell you in perfon, how much I think myfelf

Your moft obliged

humble fervant.

F I N I S.

LaVergne, TN USA
14 June 2010
186072LV00003B/38/P